ANIMAL STORIES
TRUE

Robin B. Cano
Irving Wasserman
Bee Thorpe

James Moffett, Senior Editor

Houghton Mifflin Company • Boston

Atlanta   Dallas   Geneva, Illinois   Hopewell, New Jersey   Palo Alto

Acknowledgments

Wm. Collins Sons & Co. Ltd., for "The Story of Cholmondely the Chimpanzee," adapted from *The New Noah* by Gerald Durrell. Reprinted by permission of Wm. Collins Sons & Co. Ltd.

E. P. Dutton & Co., Inc., for "Little Rascal," from the book *Little Rascal* by Sterling North, illustrated by Carl Burger. Copyright © 1965 by Sterling North, illustrations copyright © 1965 by Carl Burger. Published by E. P. Dutton & Co., Inc., text and illustrations used with their permission.

Highlights for Children, Inc., for "The Friendly Prairie Dog" by Margaret Zinn. Copyright © 1968 by Highlights for Children, Inc., Columbus, Ohio. Reprinted by permission of Highlights for Children, Inc.

Houghton Mifflin Company, for the selection entitled "A Capybara in the Family," from *Capyboppy* by Bill Peet. Copyright © 1966 by William Peet. Text and illustrations reprinted by permission of Houghton Mifflin Company.

Gladys F. Lewis, for "The Black Stallion and the Red Mare." Reprinted by permission of the author.

Little, Brown and Company, for "Food for Wolves," adapted from *Never Cry Wolf* by Farley Mowat. Copyright © 1963 by Farley Mowat. Reprinted by permission of Atlantic-Little, Brown and Co.

Little, Brown & Company (Canada) Limited, for "Food for Wolves," adapted from *Never Cry Wolf* by Farley Mowat. Reprinted by permission of Little, Brown & Company (Canada) Limited, Toronto.

The Macmillan Company, for "A Mermaid on a Dolphin's Back," from *The Secrets of the Dolphin* by Helen Kay. © Copyright by Helen Kay, 1964. Reprinted with permission of The Macmillan Company.

Helen W. Thurber, for "Snapshot of a Dog" by James Thurber, copyright © 1935 James Thurber, copyright © 1963 Helen W. Thurber and Rosemary Thurber Sauers, from *The Middle-Aged Man on the Flying Trapeze*, published by Harper and Row. Originally printed in *The New Yorker.*

The Viking Press, Inc., for "Battle by the Breadfruit Tree," adapted from *On Safari* by Theodore J. Waldeck, copyright 1940 by Theodore J. Waldeck, copyright © renewed 1968 by JoBesse McElveen Waldeck, reprinted by permission of The Viking Press, Inc. For "The Story of Cholmondely the Chimpanzee," adapted from *The New Noah* by Gerald Durrell, copyright 1953, 1954 by Gerald M. Durrell, reprinted by permission of The Viking Press, Inc.

Contents

Next, see "Keep an Animal Log" and "Write Your Own Animal Story" in FINDING OUT, "Make an Animal" and "Map a Zoo or Park" in MAKING THINGS, "Sharing Reading" in TELLING ABOUT, and "Who's Talking?" in MAKING UP.

Stories on circled ○ pages have been recorded. Look for them under *Animal Stories, True* in the LISTENING LIBRARY.

Little Rascal

by Sterling North

How do you feed a baby raccoon weighing less than one pound?

Some children feed them with a medicine dropper or a doll's nursing bottle. But I fed my tiny raccoon through a clean wheat straw. I took warm milk in my mouth, then tilted the hollow straw downward to his mouth and watched him suck eagerly.

I called my raccoon "Rascal" because he was such a mischief. He had gleaming black eyes, a mask like a little bandit, and five black rings around his fluffy tail. His whispered trills were full of wonder and curiosity. In the wide-spreading oak tree behind our house there was a comfortable hole which made a good home for Rascal. Here he dreamed away his first two months, sleeping happily between feedings.

At the foot of this great tree lay my big Saint Bernard, Wowser. He was a dependable watchdog who protected all my pets:

My little woodchucks!

My good little black-and-white skunks in their cages!

My cats of many colors!

1

And even my wicked pet crow named Poe, who liked to steal every shining object he could find and hide these treasures in the belfry of the Methodist Church.

Wowser was a handsome animal weighing one hundred and seventy pounds. It would have been a brave dog or a foolish boy who tried to disturb Wowser's new friend, my little raccoon, Rascal.

One day in June, when cherries were ripe and the whole world cheerful with bird song, Wowser and I heard a quavering trill at the hole in the tree. A moment later we saw two bright eyes shining from a small black mask. Rascal was peering from the door of his home at the world below, and soon he began backing down the tree like a little bear, tail first.

Wowser was worried. He yelped a question or two and glanced up to see what I thought about this new problem. I told my dog not to worry, but to watch what happened.

I had a shallow minnow pool not far from the tree. Rascal hurried to the little pond and started fishing. His sensitive hands searched the shallows, while his eyes gazed far away as though he were thinking of something else entirely. Soon his clever little hands caught a minnow. He began washing it back and forth as raccoons do with almost everything they eat. Rascal carried his minnow to the edge of the pool, very pleased with himself, and began eating the small fish in polite little nibbles. Then he started exploring the back yard surrounding the oak tree. Once he pounced on a cricket. A moment later he lay very still while the dark shadow of Poe-the-Crow swept across the grass. When Rascal came too near to the edge of our green lawn, Wowser pushed him back, firmly but gently.

Having explored his little world, my raccoon climbed the tree and disappeared into his safe home in the hollow of the oak. He seemed to be perfectly satisfied with his first trip abroad. Wowser sighed with relief. Rascal was again safely in his nest. He had not hurt himself nor run away. Perhaps he would not be the problem that Wowser had feared. Being a Rascal-sitter was a twenty-four-hour-a-day job.

My father and I lived alone together in a ten-room house in the little town of Brailsford Junction in southern Wisconsin. My mother was dead, and my two older sisters, Theo and Jessica, were living elsewhere. My big brother, Herschel, was with the American Army in France, fighting against the Germans in World War I.

My father was very kind to me. He let me build my canoe in the living room, keep any number of pets, and wander as free as the wind over meadows and hills. I knew that he would not object to having Rascal eat with us at the table. From the attic I carried down the family high-chair last used when I was a baby.

At breakfast next morning I put a shallow earthen-ware bowl of warm milk on the tray of the highchair. Rascal stood in the chair, placing his hands on the edge of the tray. He could reach the milk easily, and he chirred and trilled his satisfaction. He drank his milk, scarcely dribbling a drop. In fact, his table manners were better than those of many children. My father smiled fondly at our new breakfast companion, and I was delighted at Rascal's good behavior.

All went well until I offered the raccoon a lump of sugar. Rascal took it between his two hands and began washing it back and forth in his milk just as he had washed the minnow. In a moment or two, of course, it melted entirely away, and you could not imagine a more surprised little raccoon.

First he felt all over the bottom of the bowl to see if he had dropped it.

Then he looked in his right hand! No sugar lump!

Next he looked in his left hand! No sugar lump there either!

Finally he turned to me and shrilled a sharp question. Who had stolen his lump of sugar?

When I recovered from my laughter, I gave him a second lump. He thought about washing it, but then a shrewd look came into his shining eyes. He took the sugar directly to his mouth and began munching it happily.

Rascal was a very bright raccoon. When he learned a lesson, he learned it for life. Never again did he try to wash a lump of sugar.

The kitchen screen door had a worn catch and a weak spring. I did not repair them because I wanted my cats to be able to pull the door open to let themselves in, or push it from the inside to let themselves out. Rascal was certain he could do anything that a cat could do. Several times he watched them open the door. Obviously the trick was to hook your claws in the screen, and pull. Feeling very proud of himself, he showed the cats that he was as smart as the oldest and wisest Tom.

A few nights later I was surprised and delighted to hear Rascal's trill from the pillow beside me. Then I felt

his little hands exploring my face. My raccoon baby had climbed down from his hole in the tree and had opened the back screen door. With eyes that could see in the dark, he had found his way to my downstairs bedroom. There were no very strict rules in our house, as both Rascal and I realized. My raccoon decided the most comfortable place to sleep was with me. He was as clean as any cat, and perfectly housebroken from the start. So for many months we slept together.

I felt less lonesome now when my father went away on business, leaving me all alone in that big ten-room house.

From *Little Rascal* by Sterling North.

The Friendly Prairie Dog
by Margaret Zinn

One warm spring day my father was breaking sod on our new farm in Oklahoma. I was following close behind in the furrow, enjoying the feel of cool earth on my bare feet. Suddenly the plow turned up a baby prairie dog. He fell at my feet, crying pitifully.

My father stopped the team and picked him up and stroked him gently. I wanted to take him home as a new pet, but Father said he was only a baby and needed his mother. Then Father noticed that one of his hind legs was broken. With some smooth, stout sticks and strips from his pocket handkerchief, he set the broken leg. Since the little dog was injured, Father said I might take him home.

My sister and I had raised many pets and we knew how to care for him. We put a spoonful of milk in a cup and added a spoonful of hot water. My sister held the little fellow firmly in both hands while I fed him. I would hold a spoonful to his mouth and force the edge of the spoon gently between his teeth. Of course he resented this. We got much more milk on the outside than on the inside at first, but he tasted it and seemed to like it. Many times each day we gave him fresh grass and roots and a bit of warm milk. Soon he eagerly accepted the spoon and swallowed the milk.

We fixed him a warm box behind the kitchen stove. We had raised other pets in this box which we called our "nursery." When his leg had become less painful, he began venturing out of the box. At first he stayed close by it and would hurry back inside at the least sign of danger. It was then we named him Paddy, because the splint on his leg made a queer little thumping noise as he hurried along. But soon he was exploring all over the house.

Sometimes Paddy would curl up in a dark corner and could not be found. But all we needed to do was to strike a spoon against the side of a cup and he would come running. That was the dinner bell for him. The tinkle of the silver against the dinner plates always brought him too. He learned to eat nearly everything we ate. He loved cookies. But his great weakness was for cheese. He would go to any heights to get a bite of cheese.

We all loved Paddy and only laughed at the trouble he caused. His little leg had healed, and he was able to scramble up on a chair or bed.

Then one day Aunt Sarah, my father's sister, came from Kansas to visit us. We were greatly excited about having company. Paddy did not join us when we ate supper. Everyone was talking and we forgot him.

Aunt Sarah went to bed by the dim light of a lantern in our attic bedroom. I had the privilege of sleeping in the attic too, a thing I never did by myself.

I was snug in my bed and Aunt Sarah blew out the light. Suddenly she gave out a scream that shook the

rafters. She was out of bed and down the stairs in a hurry. I had no idea what was the matter, but I was right behind her when she reached the kitchen. She was shaking so much she could hardly speak. Finally she managed to say that there was an animal in her bed. I knew at once that it was Paddy.

Well, that was too much for Father. He said Paddy would have to go. But we all loved Paddy and just couldn't take him back to prairie dog town. We compromised by taking him over to the little country store across the road. The storekeeper was a good neighbor who liked animals. He agreed to let Paddy stay in the store and let us visit him whenever we wished.

Paddy was soon right at home in the store. He would scurry around the floor, picking up crumbs and begging for handouts. He always knew when cheese was sold and would come quickly.

In those days cheese was packed in big round wooden boxes. All the storekeeper needed to do to bring Paddy out was to open the cheese box. Many people would buy a few slices of cheese and a box of crackers to eat before starting home. Most everyone shared the cheese with Paddy.

But Paddy was soon to get into trouble. One day a farmer's wife bought cheese and crackers and sat down in the store to eat some. She paid no attention to the pleadings of Paddy. He became impatient and jumped to her shoulder and tried to help himself. She was greatly frightened. Then she became indignant at the thought of sharing her meal with a prairie dog and left the store in a huff. So Paddy was banished from the store.

Sorrowfully my sister and I carried Paddy out beyond
the fields to a hillside where the prairie dogs had built
their new town, and there we left him. We went often
to visit him in his new home. At the first sign of our
approach, the prairie dogs would dart into their holes. If
we were very quiet, except for tapping a spoon against a
cup, Paddy would soon appear. We would feed him all

the things he liked — cheese and cookies and bits of apple.
After a while other prairie dogs would pop up out of the
holes. They would chatter and scold but never had the
courage to follow Paddy. Often, if we left food near their
holes, they would help themselves after we were some
distance away. Paddy seemed to be quite happy in his new
home. He never lost his love for cheese.

A Capybara in the Family

by Bill Peet

Although Bill had pestered his family to let him have a boa constrictor, they would not give in. Finally they agreed that Bill could get a capybara instead.

Capybaras look something like giant guinea pigs, to which they are related. They are vegetarians and live in swamps or along riverbanks in the South American Jungles. Their thick bodies are covered with coarse brown hair. They have no tail. Their feet are partly webbed and they are good swimmers. When in captivity capybaras are known to be very friendly.

Bill's father tells about the capybara's first weeks in the Peet family.

Bill lost no time in contacting a wild-animal importer to put in his order for one capybara. That was in the middle of March. One afternoon in early April, Bill came wheeling happily home in his jeep with his new rodent friend seated beside him.

The instant the jeep pulled to a stop in front of the house the capybara was out the car door, and he came waddling up the walk, as if he understood that this was his new home. My wife Margaret, our younger son Steve, and I rushed out to greet him but he passed us by without a glance, twitching his tiny mouse ears and making a bird-like "tweetle-tweet" sound. After taking a few nibbles at the ivy he hopped onto the porch, then "tweetle-tweeted" on in the front door.

He paused in the entry hall for a brief look around, then headed into the family room where the cats were drowsing on the love seat. At the sound of the "tweetle-tweet" the cats suddenly sat up. Perhaps they expected to see a bird.

But when they spied the huge no-tailed mouse they were horrified. They exploded off the love seat "kitty-boom!" and went streaking away to the living room.

The capybara hardly noticed them. He followed his sensitive nose straight for the kitchen to the three bowls of cat food which had hardly been touched. Vegetarian though he was, the capybara seemed to enjoy the cat food. He finished off one bowl after another while the bewildered cats watched at a safe distance.

What a shock it must have been to see the old cat-
and-mouse game turned completely topsy-turvy. However, the cats hadn't seen anything yet. The big rodent
was only five or six weeks old, and was just beginning to
grow.

After finishing off the cat food he put away a heaping big bowl of oats and barley. Then the capy began exploring the house with all four of us trailing after him, curious to see how our jungle creature would take to his new surroundings.

We followed his cheery "tweetle-tweet" as he wandered in and out of the rooms, circling behind chairs, snooping under beds, and exploring every closet.

All at once we realized he was doing much more than snooping, he was sampling things for taste. To the capybara everything was edible until proven otherwise. A few quick nips and a shoe was beyond repair, "crunch!" and a wicker chair seat began to unravel, "chomp!" and a handbag strap flew apart. This was proof enough that the capy was not the ideal household pet so we promptly escorted him out to the backyard.

If we had planned the yard for the visitor from the Amazon jungle it couldn't have been more ideal. There was a swimming pool with a border of broad-leaved tropical plants, and on beyond was a sloping bank over-grown with a dense tangle of trees and shrubs; and our jungle was completely fenced in.

We watched anxiously as he sniffed the tropical plants, certain that they were doomed to the very last leaf. But after a few nibbles the capy lost interest and waddled out onto the lawn.

He found the lawn much more to his taste and he
settled down to graze, his large rodent teeth clipping off
the grass about an inch from the ground as neatly and
evenly as a lawn mower. A mower with built-in
grasscatcher that left no wheel tracks. The lawn area was
small and Capy could have finished the mowing job in
half an hour if he hadn't been distracted by the glitter
of sunlit water. And he headed for the pool.

For a moment he teetered awkwardly on the edge then toppled in "ker plosh!" Once in the water, Capy was surprisingly graceful. His broad webbed feet propelled him along in a smooth easy glide with his eyes, ears, and nose skimming over the surface.

After one leisurely cruise around the pool he hauled himself out. Swimming all alone wasn't much fun. Capy needed a few playmates and a bit of competition to show what a truly fine swimmer he was.

Bill and Steve were gone during the week to their summer jobs, but on the weekends when friends came to join them for a swim Capy was always in the thick of the action. The excitement of the shouting, splashing teenagers and small-fry brought out the show-off in the big rodent. He seemed to be everywhere, dodging in and out and under flying arms and legs and swim fins.

Nobody could outdo Capy when it came to swimming underwater, but then he had all the natural equipment such as self-sealing nostrils and ears, plus two pairs of swim fins, and he circled the pool time after time before bobbing to the surface for air.

When at last the weary waterlogged swimmers gave up, Capy gave up too. He joined his friends in the sun, adding a few of his own "tweetle-tweets" to the general conversation. For all the capybara knew, he was a teenager too, and a full-fledged member of our family.

From *Capyboppy* by Bill Peet.

OPONONI
BEACH
HOKIANGA
HARBOR
NEW
ZEALAND
TASMAN
SEA
PACIFIC
OCEAN
N
W
E
S

A Mermaid
on a Dolphin's Back
by Helen Kay

. . . once I sat upon a promontory,
And heard a mermaid on a dolphin's back
Uttering such dulcet and harmonious breath
That the rude sea grew civil at her song
And certain stars shot madly from their spheres,
To hear the sea-maid's music.

William Shakespeare, *A Midsummer Night's Dream*

Suddenly one day Jill Baker of Opononi, New Zealand, aged twelve, was turned into a mermaid — not by the wave of a magic wand, but by an odd and beautiful circumstance.

Jill Baker was a powerful swimmer. She couldn't help being one, for she lived right on the sea. Opononi Beach at Hokianga Harbor on the western side of northern New Zealand was a seaside resort. Jill needed only to cross the main road, pass a strip of sandy beach, and step into the water.

One day as she bathed in the harbor with the pink sand hills all around, she was startled by a large animal that rose out of the sea in front of her. Face to face with her, it seemed to grin. It was even staring curiously at her out of large brown eyes.

Jill was frightened . . . frightened by its size and the many teeth in its open mouth. Turning quickly about, she began to swim to safety.

The dolphin followed her — raced her, in fact. It popped up in front, then swam alongside. It leaped out of the water and circled her. Jill swam faster, but she could not outswim it. She realized the dolphin wanted to play. This, then, was the friendly dolphin she had heard about.

Jill slowed her pace, and together they glided side by side.

Measuring the animal by the length of her own body, she saw that "when swimming along beside, it did not seem very large . . . probably because the back half was nearly always under water."

By the time Jill reached shallow water, they had become good friends. When she stood up, the dolphin swam between her legs, lifted her gently and carried her out again, playfully dumped her and raced back to shore.

From that moment on, Opononi Beach was on the map of the world. Jill Baker was no longer just a New Zealand schoolgirl in a sleepy vacation town. She had been turned into a "mermaid on a dolphin's back."

The dolphin, too, was given a name, "Opo," shortened from Opononi Beach, the seaside resort that was its home for six months during the winter of 1955–1956, which is summer "down under" in New Zealand.

Beyond the beach lived the farmers and fishermen — many of them Maori, the original inhabitants of New Zealand.

One farmer, Piwai Toi, described how he had met the friendly dolphin for the first time: "There was a splash and a boiling swirl, and a large fish was streaking for my boat just under the surface. I really thought it was going to hit us, when about ten yards away it dived and surfaced on the other side. It played round and round the boat. I was afraid she would be hit by my outboards, so I went inshore. . . . When I looked back . . . she was about three feet out of the water, standing literally on her tail, and looking at me from a distance of about fifty yards. . . ."*

Opo continued to look at the people at Opononi Beach, and the people on the beach looked back.

* *Te Ao Hou*, The Maori Magazine, Wellington, New Zealand

They came by the hundreds and they came by the thousands. By Christmas of 1955, the weekends saw as many as two thousand people looking for Jill Baker's friend, Opo. They filled the one hotel and overflowed the pine-tree motor camp. Then they slept in their cars or on the beach. They came on foot, by bicycle, motor scooter, boat, car, bus, van, truck, any way they could — to see the friendly fish.

Mothers with children — whole families — arrived to picnic and look for Opo. Up and down the shore they waited.

If Opo was not there yet, boatmen called her from her fishing coves by starting their motors. The "putt putt putt" of the motors brought her with a swish and a swirl, a dive and a leap, full of the sheer joy of living.

That season Opo was the star of Opononi Beach. Even the experts came to see.

A zoologist announced that Opo of Opononi was indeed a bottle-nosed dolphin, *Tursiops truncatus*, and was almost fully grown. "This is no fish," he said, "but an aquatic mammal."

What sex?

No one was sure. Most thought Opo must be female since she was so gentle with children. Opo would swim right among them to join their games. "Ketch and fetch" was her favorite; next came "water polo" and "ring-around-a-porpoise."

From the very first moment Opo was thrown a ball, she showed she was a champion. She couldn't catch with her stubby flippers. They were too short, equivalent only to mittened hands without the stretch of arms behind them. But her mouth was large, and fine for grasping. With the ball in her mouth, she began to play. She dribbled it in the water; carefully she balanced it on her blunt snout. Then she sent it spinning twenty feet in the air. Before it reached the sea again, Opo was under it for the catch. All alone, she was an all-star team.

"And," said Jill Baker, "she was never *taught* any of these tricks."

The people were excited by the daring dolphin. Some ran into the sea, still wearing all their clothes. They were like the children: they wanted to get close, touch her, pinch her. "Is she real?" They needed to make sure.

As the season reached its peak, Opo showed even greater talent. She rolled the ball down her back, then hit it sideways, using her tail or dorsal fin like a bat. Sometimes she would turn upside down, showing a round white belly, clutching a big red ball between those stubby flippers.

"Opo loved to play best of all in the evening when most of the crowds had gone home. One of her favorite tricks was to find an empty bottle at the bottom of the sea and toss it into the air, then catch it with her tail. She would get quite excited and start snorting like a pig," Jill Baker said.

"Sometimes while playing with the people, she would follow them right onto the edge of the beach, and would of course get stranded. She would then have to be helped out again into deeper water."

Opo enjoyed those games, but she liked Jill even better than playing ball.

Jill thought it was because she was so gentle with her. She touched Opo kindly, lightly. She understood that Opo had a tender skin. She learned Opo liked to be tickled and scratched like a kitten. She scratched her on the top

of her head or under her throat. She would put her arms around Opo and marvel at her skin's smooth coolness.

How did it feel to ride Opo?

Jill Baker answered: "Riding Opo felt like riding a rolling piece of floating wood, because you wouldn't know when you were going to fall off."

When Opo did not see her friend on the shore, or was suddenly bored with playing ball, or became hungry, she would splash all with a flip of her tail and swim off to fish in the quiet bays on the other side of the harbor. Opo had to eat, and she had to catch her own food. She never took food from her human friends, though she spent whole days playing with them.

There were some who hit Opo too hard in their enthusiasm, yet Opo never hit back. No one was ever hurt by Opo. She did butt some on the shins; she did dig curiously under wiggling toes with her snout, but she did not bite a single adult or child. She had the teeth to do it with — there were one hundred in her mouth. And she had the strength to hurt — Opo already weighed two hundred pounds. She also had the provocation.

"Opo did not like being grabbed by her dorsal fin or her tail, as I think they were both very tender," Jill Baker said.

Once a boat hurt Opo. The propellers from a fishing smack scraped her side. The bleeding dolphin raced out to sea, and all Opononi worried. Would she come back?

That was an anxious night at Opononi Beach.

Next morning a reassuring shout went up as Opo returned with a leap and a dive: "She's all right!"

And the people kept coming. They came from nearby towns and villages. They came from the big cities, too.

Little children mispronounced "dolphin" and coined a new name for Opo. They called her "Golphin." So a sign was posted on the road, a plea to visitors: "Welcome to Opononi, but don't try to shoot our Golphin."

The newspaper photographers found Opo photogenic, but a fine way to waste film. They complained Opo liked to nuzzle so close that they couldn't shoot a good picture. One photographer thought Opo was in love with his bright blue swimming trunks. He couldn't get her away from them.

"She was a lovely creature, very gentle with children," Jill said, remembering how patiently the dolphin waited as Jill mounted small children on her back.

One day a teacher brought the whole class to the beach for a picnic. Twelve small schoolchildren went into two feet of water and formed a circle. The dolphin swam into the middle; the children threw a bright red ball and Opo tossed it high.

She stayed in the center of that ring as though she had been trained to do so. Never had there been such a picnic. Where in all the oceans had a wild dolphin joined a school of children?

One afternoon Opo did not return from fishing.

The people of Opononi Beach did not worry at first. Perhaps she needed to fish longer? Some fishermen thought the dolphin was already spending too much time playing and not enough time eating. If Opo played for as long as six hours a day, she could not eat during that time. While all eyes were looking for Opo, the fishermen

thought: "Perhaps she is catching her supper, making up for lost eating time."

But she was missing all the next day, too.

Jill Baker watched the horizon with the others.

The fishermen started up their motors. The "putt putt putt" did not bring Opo back.

On the third day Don Boyce, a farmer, was out collecting mussels, and he found her. She was jammed between large rocks on the southern side of the harbor about three miles from the village. Opo was dead. The people thought they knew how it had happened:

She had been catching fish when the tide went out. Suddenly a prisoner in a rocky crevice, she struggled to escape. But she had no hands or feet to maneuver, and without water to hold her up, she thrashed her body against the rough rock edges and cut herself to shreds.

Perhaps she bled to death trying to free herself? Or she drowned when the tide came in, imprisoned by the rocks, too exhausted to hold her blowhole above water?

Drowned? You might wonder: can a dolphin drown?

On Saturday, as the weekend crowds were coming, a boat brought Opo's body back to Opononi Beach. All on shore seemed to know. It was a gloomy day, though the sun still shone when she was brought onto the beach and laid gently on the sand.

The flag on the Memorial Hall was lowered. The postmistress of Opononi said, "This is a sad, sad place," as she read a telegram from the people at the Auckland War Memorial Museum. They wanted a plaster cast of Opo, and were sending a staff member to determine Opo's sex, species, and other scientific data.

When the man from the museum arrived, he said that Opo was a female dolphin, a *Tursiops truncatus*, about a year and a half in age. She was a young dolphin, a playful puppy still.

They made the plaster cast to take to the Auckland Museum, and only then was Opo buried near the Memorial Hall.

The children came with bouquets for her grave, covering it with wild flowers from the pink sand hills.

"I was home at the time she died, and couldn't really believe it at first," Jill said. "I think she was almost too good to be true."

The editor of the Maori magazine *Te Ao Hou* has given me the true facts about Opo's death. Three young boys had accidentally killed the dolphin when they were dynamiting for fish in the middle of Hokianga Harbor. Horrified at what they had done, they put Opo's body in the rocky crevice, to be found later by Don Boyce. They were just as tearful as the rest of the people of Opononi Beach — knowing their foolishness had killed Opononi's prize.

Sculptor Russell Clark was so moved by Opo's death that he carved a statue out of fawn-colored Hinuera stone in her memory. With Opo, the friendly dolphin, stands a small Maori boy. Jill Baker described the statue: "The stone carving of Opo is about six feet long. The boy has his arm resting on Opo. The boy represents the children who played with her. They are both in the water with waves all around. At the moment, the statue is standing on her grave in front of the Memorial Hall, but it is only in a temporary position."

To the question "Why did Opo choose you, Jill Baker, among all the others at Opononi Beach as a friend?" Jill answered that she thought she knew the secret of her popularity with Opo:

"Opo was always nearby when I went in for a swim. I used to wear blue flippers, and I think she took a fancy to them."

Jill Baker has grown to womanhood, but she will never forget the dolphin who made her a mermaid in the twentieth century.

From *The Secrets of the Dolphin* by Helen Kay.

Battle by the Breadfruit Tree
by Theodore J. Waldeck

Famous explorer Theodore Waldeck and his partner, Albert Smith, have gone to the big game areas of Kenya, in east-central Africa, to take motion pictures of wild animals in their natural surroundings.

Smith and I were anxious to take motion pictures of a herd of baboons. We had tried and tried, with no success whatever, though we saw many of these creatures. Our camp was some miles from a little ravine through which a stream ran. Beyond the ravine was a plateau leading back to thick woods. The baboons, scores of them, came out of these woods with their young to play on the plateau and to drink from the stream. Often Smith and I watched them, tried to photograph them, but could never get close enough. The baboons enjoyed what we were doing. They thought it was a game of some sort.

Once we set up the camera at the edge of the plateau, in order to take them when they came through the woods at dawn to greet the sun. We didn't even come close, for when the baboons saw us, they charged like a shrieking

45

army of savages. They threw sticks and stones at us, and we fled as though the devil and all his imps were at our heels. A grown bull baboon could have torn either of us to shreds. We didn't even stop to take our camera. We felt sure that our camera would be a wreck when we returned — which could not be until the baboons had retired from the plateau. We went back then, to find it exactly as we had left it. They had not so much as touched it.

"We *must* get those pictures," said Smith, "and I think I know the answer. Those breadfruit trees this side of the ravine. That big one, with the leafy top. . . ."

"Yes?"

"We'll go there now and build a platform up among the leaves, set up our camera, take blankets and a thermos bottle filled with hot tea, and spend the night. Then, when they come out in the morning, we'll be looking right down on them."

I saw that he was right, and we set about it. The trekkers got boards from the camp and carried them to the tree. Big limbs were cut off and lashed high among the leaves at the top of the breadfruit tree. Then the boards were laid across the limbs and the camera set up. We had supper, took our blankets, and went to the tree to spend an uncomfortable night; but however uncomfortable it might be, it would not matter if we got our pictures.

Night. We sat hunched up with our blankets over us listening to the sounds of the night. Now and again we dozed off. Then we'd awaken. I'd have a cigarette; Smith would smoke his pipe. The wind blew steadily toward us from the plateau, which could see dimly in the moonlight. The hours wore on.

Finally, animals began to greet the growing morning, though it would be some time, if they stuck to schedule, before the baboons appeared. I sat back on my blanket now — it was already warm enough to do without it — and watched the day break. I never tired of doing that. The sun comes up in a different way in Africa. First the leaves are black. Then a grayish haze outlines their shapes. Then the gray lightens into the green of the leaves. Then the sun itself strikes through and morning is with us, covering that part of Africa with a mixture of colors. Sunlight plays upon colors like a mighty organist upon the keys, and the keys are everything the sunlight touches. It is music made visible — not just the music that men play, but the music of Nature herself, with all the sounds that Nature uses.

I sighed and drank it in. Smith was looking out through the leaves, watching for the baboons to appear. Then he nudged me, and I made an end, for the moment, of dreaming. I parted the leaves in utter silence, making sure that my lens was uncovered and aimed at the plateau, and looked through. The baboon herd had not come, but a single baboon and her baby had. Smith had not actually seen her coming. One moment he had been watching, seeing nothing. Then he had blinked his eyes and she was there. He signaled me to start the camera. I noted that the wind was toward me. I felt sure that the rest of the baboons would come, following these two. The mother baboon, while her baby played across the plateau behind her, came down to its edge to peer into the ravine, perhaps to dash down for a drink. I started the camera. It was almost silent, but not quite. And with the first whirring sound, which we ourselves could scarcely hear, though we were right beside it, the mother jumped up and looked around. Her ears had caught the little sound. She looked in all directions, twisting her head swiftly, and even in this her eyes kept darting to her young one. I stilled the whirring. We did not move or make a sound, even a whisper. She was so close we could see her nose wrinkling as she tried to get our scent. But the wind was toward us, and she got nothing. She even looked several times at the breadfruit tree that hid us.

I was about to start grinding again when a terrific squall came from the baby. It caught at my heart, that sound. I know it caught at the heart of Smith, too, for I could see it in his face. The mother baboon whirled around so fast one could scarcely see the movement. The baby was jumping swiftly to the top of a rock, which was all too low to be of any use to him as protection against the creature that was close behind him.

That creature was a hunting leopard, or cheetah, and it, like the baboon, had come so softly and silently that we had not seen it. It was simply there, a murderous

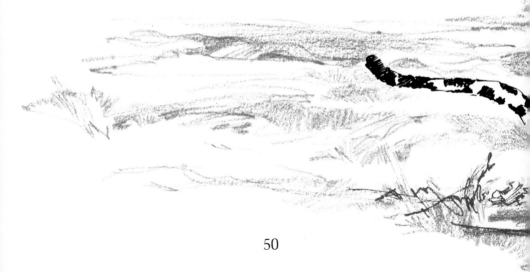

streak behind the baby baboon. Did the female hesitate for a single moment? Not at all. If the leopard was a streak, so was the mother baboon. She shot toward that leopard and was in the air above him, reaching for his neck, while he was in mid-leap behind the baby, which now sat upon the rock and uttered doleful screams of terror.

The great cat instantly had his work cut out for him. For the baboon, by gripping his neck from behind, beyond reach of those talons, could break it. And that was what she tried, with hands and feet and killing incisors. But while I knew nothing of this fighting combination, the leopard must have, for he did what any cat would instinctively do in such a case. He spun to his back and reached for the baboon with all four of his brutally armed paws. One stroke across the abdomen of the baboon and she would be killed outright. But she knew something of leopards.

Smith did not make a sound, nor did I. I don't think we even breathed. The great cat recovered himself as the baboon jumped free of the leopard and ran toward her baby. The leopard charged the baboon. The baboon waited until the last minute, shot into the air, allowed the cat to go under her, turned in the air, and dropped back for the killing hold on the back of the neck again.

She got some hair in her mouth, which she spat out disgustedly. The baby kept on squalling. As nearly as I could tell — though I probably would not have heard even the trumpeting of elephants or the roaring of lions — there was no sound other than the screaming of the female baboon, the squalling of her baby, and the spitting and snarling of the leopard.

This time, when the leopard whirled to his back to dislodge the baboon, he managed to sink his claws into her. I saw the blood spurt from the baboon's body, dyeing her fur. I knew that the smell of blood would drive the leopard mad, and it did. He would just as soon eat the meat of a grown baboon if he could not have the baby.

Both stood off for a second, regarding each other, to spit out fur and hair. Then the leopard charged once more. Again the baboon leaped high and then started down, reaching for that neck. And this time, when she came down, the leopard had already turned, and she could not entirely avoid landing among those fearful talons. Even a baboon could not jump from a spot in mid-air. For a brief moment there was a terrific flurry of in-fighting, from which came the snarling of the leopard, the screaming of the she-baboon. Now we could see the leopard, now the baboon, the latter trying with all her strength and agility to escape a fatal stroke from one of the four feet of the killer. Then both were so mixed up, fighting all over the plateau, that we could not distinguish them. We could tell they were together because they formed a ball of fighting fury, and the sounds of the two animals came out of the pinwheel of murderous action.

How long it lasted I do not know. To the she-baboon and her baby it must have seemed ages. It may have been seconds, even a minute. And then they were standing off, catching their breath, spitting out fur, regarding each other again. Both were tired. To my utter amazement the baboon was holding her own with the leopard. At that moment I would not have known which one had the edge, if either. For both were panting, weary, and stained with blood.

Neither gave ground. By common consent they stood for a few seconds, the baboon on her hind legs, the leopard crouching on all fours. Then the leopard charged. Again the baboon went into the air to let the leopard go under her. She knew better, at this stage of the game, than to run away or jump to either side. The leopard could over-take her if she ran, or could turn instantly and follow her if she jumped to either side. So up and over was her only chance. Again she came down. But this time she was expecting the cat to whip upon his back and present his talons, and she was ready. She twisted aside a little, and to the front, perhaps with some idea of reaching for the neck from the underside, now uppermost. The forepaws of the leopard lashed at her. The sun gleamed on the exposed talons and showed that they were red with baboon blood. I could see long welts across the abdomen of the baboon. She had evaded those slashes at the last moment, each time. Feeling the talons' touch, she had got away just enough to escape disemboweling, not enough to escape deep, parallel gashes that reached inward for her life.

Now I began to see how the fight was going to go, though neither Smith nor I could have done anything about it, because we were spellbound, rooted to our place in the breadfruit tree, watching something that few explorers had ever seen: a battle between a leopard and a baboon! And for the best reason in the world — the baboon to protect her baby.

But now the she-baboon was tiring. It was obvious in all her movements, though I knew and the leopard knew that as long as she stood upright and could see him, she was dynamite — fury incarnate, capable of slaying if she got in the blows she wanted. So far she had not made it.

Now she panted more than the leopard did. She did not entirely evade his rushes, though she jumped over him as before. But she did not go as high or twist as quickly in the air. She couldn't. Her body was beginning to weigh too much for her tiring muscles. She was like

an arm-weary prize fighter who had almost fought himself out. But her little eyes still glared defiance; her screaming still informed him that she was ready for more. Now there were other slashes upon her face, her head, her chest, and her abdomen — clear down even to her hands and feet. But she never even thought of quitting. They drew apart once more, spitting fur. They glared at each other. Several times I saw the orange eyes of the leopard, and in them were hate and fury and thwarted hunger.

Now he charged before the baboon had rested enough. He was getting stronger, the baboon weaker. His second wind came sooner perhaps, and he sorely needed it. Even yet the baboon could break his neck, given the one chance.

Again the baboon went into the air, came down, and was caught in the midst of those four paws. Again the battle raged, the two animals all mixed up together, all over the plateau. The little one squalled from his boulder, and there was despair in his voice. He cried hopeless encouragement to his mother. She heard — I knew she did — and tried to find some reserve with which to meet the attacks of the killer.

That last piece of in-fighting lasted almost too long. There was no relief from it, and the nerves of the two men who watched were strained to the breaking point, though neither was aware of it. How long they had held their breath they did not know.

The two beasts broke apart, and I saw instantly that the leopard had at last succeeded, managing the stroke he had been trying for since the battle began. He had raked deeply into the abdomen of the baboon. The result may be well imagined. The baboon drew off slowly and looked down at herself. What she saw told her the truth — that even if the leopard turned and ran away this minute, she was done.

But did she expect mercy? Death did not grant mercy in Africa — certainly not on this particular morning.

The baboon noted the direction of the leopard's glance. The great cat was crouched well back, but facing the rock on which the baby squalled. He licked his chops, looked at the dying she-baboon, and growled; and it was as though he said: "Not much time now. And when you are gone, nothing will keep me from getting him!"

As if the leopard had actually screamed those words, I got the thought which raced through his evil head. And the baboon got it, too. For she turned slowly, like a dead thing walking, and moved to turn her back toward the rock, so that the baby was almost over her head.

Then she looked at the leopard once more and screamed, as though she answered: "Perhaps, but over my dead body!"

The leopard charged again, for the last time. It would be easy now. And as the she-baboon set herself against that last charge, the strangest, most nearly human cry I ever heard went keening out across the veldt. It bounced against the breadfruit trees and dipped into the ravine; it went back through the forest whence the other baboons usually came to play and drink. It went out in all directions, that cry, across the plain. It rolled across the mounded hills. It was a cry that could never be forgotten by those that heard it.

And then, in the midst of the cry — like none she had uttered while the fight had been so fierce — the leopard struck her down. She sprawled, beaten to a pulp, at the base of the boulder, while that last cry of hers still moved across the veldt.

And now, sure that the she-baboon was dead, the leopard backed away, crouched, lifted his eyes to the baby on the rock.

I came to life then, realizing for the first time what I was seeing. I couldn't have moved before. But now, somehow, my rifle was in my hands, at my shoulder, and I was getting the leopard in my sights. Why had I not done it before and saved the life of the mother? I'll never know. Certainly, and sincerely, I had not allowed the fight to continue simply in order to see which would win out. I had simply become a statue, possessing only eyes and ears.

I got the leopard in my sights as he crouched to spring. I had his head for a target. I'd get him before he moved, before he sprang. The baby — looking down, sorrow in his cries, with a knowledge of doom, too — had nowhere to go. I tightened the trigger. And then —

At that instant the leopard was blotted out, and for several seconds I could not understand what had

happened, what the mother's last cry had meant. But now I did. For living baboons, leaping, screaming, had appeared out of nowhere. They came, the whole herd of them, and the leopard was invisible in their midst. I did not even hear the leopard snarl and spit. I heard nothing save the baboons, saw nothing save the big blur of their bodies, over and around the spot where I'd last seen the leopard.

How long that lasted I do not know. But when it was over, another mother baboon jumped to the rock, gathered up the baby, and was gone. After her trailed all the other baboons. Smith and I looked at each other, and if my face was as white and shocked as his, it was white and shocked indeed. Without a word, because we both understood, we slipped down from the tree, crossed the ravine, climbed its far side, crossed the plateau, looked down at the dead she-baboon, then looked away again.

One mother had fought to the death for the life of her baby and had saved that life. We looked around for the leopard who had slain her. We couldn't find a piece of it as big as an average man's hand. So the baboons had rallied to the dying cry of the mother baboon.

We went slowly back to the tree, got our camera down, returned with it to our camp. Not until we were back did we realize that neither of us, from the beginning of that fight to its grim and savage end, had thought of the camera, much less touched it.

One of the greatest fights any explorer ever saw was unrecorded.

From *On Safari* by Theodore J. Waldeck.

Snapshot of a Dog
by James Thurber

I ran across a dim photograph of him the other day, going through some old things. He's been dead twenty-five years. His name was Rex (my two brothers and I named him when we were in our early teens) and he was a bull terrier. "An American bull terrier," we used to say, proudly; none of your English bulls. He had one brindle eye that sometimes made him look like a clown and sometimes reminded you of a politician with derby hat and cigar. The rest of him was white except for a brindle saddle that always seemed to be slipping off and a brindle stocking on a hind leg. Nevertheless, there was a nobility about him. He was big and muscular and beautifully made. He never lost his dignity even when trying to accomplish the extravagant tasks my brothers and myself used to set for him. One of these was the bringing of a ten-foot wooden rail into the yard through the back gate. We would throw it out into the alley and tell him to go get it. Rex was as powerful as a wrestler, and there were not many things that he couldn't manage somehow to get hold of with his great jaws and lift or drag to wherever he wanted to put them, or wherever we wanted them put. He could catch the rail at the balance and lift it clear of the ground and trot with great confidence toward the gate. Of course, since the gate was only four feet wide or so, he couldn't bring the rail in broadside. He found that out when he got a few terrific jolts, but he wouldn't give up. He finally figured out how to do it, by dragging the rail, holding on to one end, growling. He got a great, wagging satisfaction out of his work. We used to bet kids who had never seen Rex in action that he could catch a baseball thrown as high as they could throw it. He almost never let us down. Rex could hold a baseball with ease in his mouth, in one cheek, as if it were a chew of tobacco.

He was a tremendous fighter, but he never started fights. I don't believe he liked to get into them, despite the fact that he came from a line of fighters. He never went for another dog's throat but for one of its ears (that teaches a dog a lesson), and he would get his grip, close his eyes, and hold on. He could hold on for hours. His longest fight lasted from dusk until amost pitch-dark, one Sunday. It was fought in East Main Street in Columbus with a large, snarly mongrel. When Rex finally got his ear grip, the brief whirlwind of snarling turned to screeching. It was frightening to listen to and to watch. The mongrel's owner boldly picked the dogs up somehow and began swinging them around his head, and finally let them fly like a hammer in a hammer throw, but although they landed ten feet away with a great plump, Rex still held on.

The two dogs eventually worked their way to the middle of the car tracks, and after a while two or three streetcars were held up by the fight. A motorman tried

to pry Rex's jaws open with a switch rod; somebody
lighted a fire and made a torch of a stick and held that
to Rex's tail, but he paid no attention. In the end, all the
residents and storekeepers in the neighborhood were on
hand, shouting this, suggesting that. Rex's joy of battle,
when battle was joined, was almost tranquil. He had a
kind of pleasant expression during fights, not a vicious
one, his eyes closed in what would have seemed to be

sleep had it not been for the turmoil of the struggle. The Oak Street Fire Department finally had to be sent for — I don't know why nobody thought of it sooner. Five or six pieces of apparatus arrived, followed by a battalion chief. A hose was attached and a powerful stream of water was turned on the dogs. Rex held on for several moments more while the torrent buffeted him about like a log in a freshet. He was a hundred yards away from where the fight started when he finally let go.

The story of that Homeric fight got all around town, and some of our relatives looked upon the incident as a blot on the family name. They insisted that we get rid of Rex, but we were very happy with him, and nobody could have made us give him up. We would have left town with him first, along any road there was to go. It would have been different, perhaps, if he'd ever started fights, or looked for trouble. But he had a gentle disposition. He never bit a person in the ten strenuous years that he lived, nor ever growled at anyone except prowlers. He killed cats, that is true, but quickly and neatly and without especial malice, the way men kill certain animals. It was the only thing he did that we could never cure him of doing. He never killed, or even chased, a squirrel. I don't know why. He had his own philosophy about such things. He never ran barking after wagons or automobiles. He didn't seem to see the idea in pursuing something you couldn't catch, or something you couldn't do anything with, even if you did catch it. A wagon was one of the things he couldn't tug along with his mighty jaws, and he knew it. Wagons, therefore, were not a part of his world.

Swimming was his favorite recreation. The first time he ever saw a body of water (Alum Creek), he trotted nervously along the steep bank for a while, fell to barking wildly, and finally plunged in from a height of eight feet or more. I shall always remember that shining, virgin dive. Then he swam upstream and back just for the pleasure of it, like a man. It was fun to see him battle upstream against a stiff current, struggling and growling every foot of the way. He had as much fun in the water as any person I have known. You didn't have to throw a stick in the water to get him to go in. Of course, he would bring back a stick to you if you did throw one in. He would even have brought back a piano if you had thrown one in.

That reminds me of the night, way after midnight, when he went a-roving in the light of the moon and brought back a small chest of drawers that he found some-where — how far from the house nobody ever knew; since it was Rex, it could easily have been half a mile. There were no drawers in the chest when he got it home, and it wasn't a good one — he hadn't taken it out of anybody's house; it was just an old cheap piece that somebody had abandoned on a trash heap. Still, it was something he wanted, probably because it presented a nice problem in transportation. It tested his mettle. We first knew about his achievement when, deep in the night, we heard him trying to get the chest up onto the porch. It sounded as if two or three people were trying to tear the house down.

We came downstairs and turned on the porch light. Rex was on the top step trying to pull the thing up, but it had caught somehow and he was just holding his own. I suppose he would have held his own till dawn if we hadn't helped him. The next day we carted the chest miles away and threw it out. If we had thrown it out in a nearby alley, he would have brought it home again, as a small token of his integrity in such matters. After all, he had been taught to carry heavy wooden objects about, and he was proud of his prowess.

I am glad Rex never saw a trained police dog jump. He was just an amateur jumper himself, but the most daring and tenacious I have ever seen. He would take on any fence we pointed out to him. Six feet was easy for him, and he could do eight by making a tremendous leap and hauling himself over finally by his paws, grunting and straining; but he lived and died without knowing that twelve- and sixteen-foot walls were too much for him. Frequently, after letting him try to go over one for a while, we would have to carry him home. He would never have given up trying.

There was in his world no such thing as the impossible. Even death couldn't beat him down. He died, it is true, but only, as one of his admirers said, after "straight-arming the death angel" for more than an hour. Late one afternoon he wandered home, too slowly and too uncertainly to be the Rex that had trotted briskly homeward up our avenue for ten years. I think we all knew when he came through the gate that he was dying. He had apparently taken a terrible beating, probably from the owner of some dog that he had got into a fight with. His head and body were scarred. His heavy collar with the teeth marks of many a battle on it was awry; some of the big brass studs in it were sprung loose from the leather. He licked at our hands and, staggering, fell, but got up again. We could see that he was looking for someone. One of his three masters was not home. He did not get home for an hour. During that hour the bull terrier fought against death as he had fought against the cold, strong current of Alum Creek, as he had fought to climb twelve-foot walls. When the person he was waiting for did come through the gate, whistling, ceasing to whistle, Rex walked a few wobbly paces toward him, touched his hand with his muzzle, and fell down again. This time he didn't get up.

The Story of Cholmondely*
the Chimpanzee
by Gerald Durrell

The author, Gerald Durrell, has been collecting wild animals in the British Cameroons, an area in west-central Africa that is now divided between the countries of Nigeria and Cameroon.

When Cholmondely, the chimpanzee, joined the collection, he immediately became the uncrowned king of it, not only because of his size, but also because he was so remarkably intelligent. Cholmondely had been the pet of a District Officer who, wanting to send the ape to the London zoo and hearing that I was collecting wild animals in that region of Africa and would shortly be returning to England, wrote and asked me if I would mind taking Cholmondely with me and handing him over to the zoo authorities. I wrote back to say that, as I already had a large collection of monkeys, another chimpanzee would not make any difference, so I would gladly escort

* (chum′lē)

Cholmondely back to England. I imagined that he would be quite a young chimp, perhaps two years old, and standing about two feet high. When he arrived I got a considerable shock.

A small van drew up outside the camp one morning and in the back of it was an enormous wooden crate. It was big enough, I thought, to house an elephant. I wondered what on earth could be inside, and when the driver told me that it contained Cholmondely I remember thinking how silly his owner was to send such a small chimpanzee in such a huge crate. I opened the door and looked inside and there sat Cholmondely. One glance at him and I realized that this was no baby chimpanzee but a fully grown one about eight or nine years old. Sitting hunched up in the dark crate, he looked as though he were about twice as big as me, and from the expression on his face I gathered that the trip had not been to his liking. Before I could shut the door of the box, however, Cholmondely had extended a long, hairy arm, clasped my hand in his, and shaken it warmly. Then he turned round and gathered up a great length of chain (one end of which was fastened to a collar round his neck), draped it carefully over his arm, and stepped down out of the box. He stood there for a moment and, after surveying me carefully, examined the camp with great interest, whereupon he held out his hand, looking at me inquiringly. I took it in mine and we walked into the tent together.

Cholmondely immediately seated himself on one of the chairs by the camp table, dropped his chain on the floor and sat back and crossed his legs. He gazed around the tent for a few minutes with a rather haughty expression on his face, and evidently deciding that it would do he turned and looked at me inquiringly again. Obviously,

he wanted me to offer him something after his tiring
journey. I had been warned before he arrived that he was
a hardened tea drinker, and so I called out to the cook
and told him to make a pot of tea. Then I went out and
had a look in Cholmondely's crate, and in the bottom I
found an enormous and very battered tin mug. When I
returned to the tent with this, Cholmondely was quite
overjoyed and even praised me for my cleverness in
finding it by uttering a few cheerful "hoo hoo" noises.

While we were waiting for the tea to arrive, I sat
down opposite Cholmondely and lit a cigarette. To my
surprise, he became very excited and held out his hand
across the table to me. Wondering what he would do, I

handed him the cigarette packet. He opened it, took out a cigarette and put it between his lips. He then reached out his hand again and I gave him the matches; to my astonishment, he took one out of the box, struck it, lit his cigarette and threw the box down on the table. Lying back in his chair he blew out clouds of smoke in the most professional manner. No one had told me that Cholmondely smoked. I wondered rather anxiously what other bad habits he might have which his master had not warned me about.

Just at that moment, the tea was brought in and Cholmondely greeted its appearance with loud and expressive hoots of joy. He watched me carefully while I half filled his mug with milk and then added the tea. I had

been told that he had a very sweet tooth, so I put in six large spoons of sugar, an action which he greeted with grunts of satisfaction. He placed his cigarette on the table and seized the mug with both hands; then he stuck out his lower lip very carefully and dipped it into the tea to make sure it was not too hot. As it was a trifle warm, he sat there blowing on it vigorously until it was cool enough, and then he drank it all down without stopping once. When he had drained the last drops, he peered into the mug and scooped out all the sugar he could with his forefinger. After that, he tipped the mug up on his nose and sat with it like that for about five minutes until the very last of the sugar had trickled down into his mouth.

I had Cholmondely's big box placed some distance away from the tent, and fixed the end of his chain to a large tree stump. He was too far away, I thought, to make a nuisance of himself but near enough to be able to watch everything that went on and to conduct long conversations with me in his "hoo hoo" language. But on the day of his arrival he caused trouble almost as soon as I had fixed him to his tree stump. Outside the tent were a lot of small, tame monkeys tied on long strings attached to stakes driven into the ground. They were about ten in number, and over them I had constructed a palm-leaf roof as a shelter from the sun. As Cholmondely was examining his surroundings, he noticed these monkeys, some eating fruit and others lying asleep in the sun, and decided he would have a little underarm pitching practice. I was working inside the tent when all at once I heard the most terrific uproar going on outside. The monkeys were screaming and chattering with rage, and I rushed out to see what had happened. Cholmondely, apparently, had picked up a rock the size of a cabbage and hurled it at

the smaller monkeys, luckily missing them all, but frightening them out of their wits. If one of them had been hit by such a big rock, it would have been killed instantly.

Just as I arrived on the scene, Cholmondely had picked up another stone and was swinging it backwards and forwards like a professional ball player, taking better aim. He was annoyed at having missed all the monkeys with his first shot. I grabbed a stick and hurried towards him, shouting, and, to my surprise, Cholmondely dropped the rock and put his arms over his head, and started to roll on the ground and scream. In my haste, I had picked up a very small twig and this made no impression on him at all, for his back was as broad and as hard as a table.

I gave him two sharp cuts with this silly little twig and followed it up with a serious scolding. He sat there picking bits of leaf off his fur and looking very guilty. I set to work and cleared away all the rocks and stones near his box, and, giving him another scolding, went back to my work. I hoped that this telling-off might have some effect on him, but when I looked out of the tent some time later, I saw him digging in the earth, presumably in search of more ammunition.

With snakes, though, Cholmondely was not nearly so brave. If he saw me handling one, he would get very agitated, wringing his hands and moaning with fear, and if I put the reptile on the ground and it started to crawl toward him, he would run to the very end of his chain and scream loudly for help, throwing bits of stick and grass at the snake to try and stop it coming any closer.

One night, I went to shut him up in his box as usual, and, to my surprise, he flatly refused to go into it. His bed of banana leaves was nicely made, and so I thought he was simply being naughty, but when I started to scold him, he took me by the hand, led me up to his box and left me there while he retreated to the safety of the end of his chain, and stood watching me anxiously. I realized there must be something inside of which he was frightened, and when I cautiously investigated I found a very small snake coiled up in the center of his bed. After I had captured it, I found that it was a harmless type; Cholmondely, of course, could not tell the difference, and he was taking no chances.

Not long after his arrival at the camp, Cholmondely, to my alarm, fell ill. For nearly two weeks he went off his food, refusing even the most tempting fruit and other delicacies, and even rejecting his daily ration of tea, a most unheard-of occurrence. All he had was a few sips of water every day, and gradually he grew thinner and thinner, his eyes sank into their sockets, and I really thought he was going to die. He lost all interest in life and sat hunched up in his box all day with his eyes closed. It was very bad for him to spend all day moping in this fashion, so in the evenings, just before the sun went down, when it was cool, I used to make him come out for walks with me. These walks were only short, and we had to rest every few yards, for Cholmondely was weak with lack of food.

One evening, just before I took him out for a walk, I filled my pockets with a special kind of biscuit that he had been very fond of. We went slowly up to the top of a small hill just beyond the camp and then sat there to admire the view. As we rested, I took a biscuit out of my pocket and ate it, smacking my lips with enjoyment, but not offering any to Cholmondely. He looked very surprised, for he knew that I always shared my food with him when we were out together. I ate a second biscuit and he watched me closely to see if I enjoyed it as much as the first. When he saw that I did, he dipped his hand into my pocket, pulled out a biscuit, smelled it suspiciously, and then, to my delight, ate it up and started looking for another. I knew then that he was going to get better. The next morning he drank a mugful of sweet tea

and ate seventeen biscuits, and for three days lived entirely on this diet. After this his appetite returned with a rush, and for the next fortnight he ate twice as much as he had ever done before, and cost me a small fortune in bananas.

Cholmondely was so quick at learning tricks and so willing to show off that when he returned to England, he became quite famous and even made several appearances on television, delighting the audiences by sitting on a chair, with a hat on, taking a cigarette and lighting it for himself, pouring out and drinking a glass of beer, and many other things. I think he must have become rather swollen-headed with his success, for not long after this he managed to escape from the zoo and went wandering off by himself through Regent's Park, much to the horror of everyone he met. On reaching the main road, he found

a bus standing there and promptly climbed aboard, for he loved being taken for a ride. The passengers, however, decided they would rather not travel by that particular bus if Cholmondely was going to use it as well, and they were all struggling to get out when some keepers arrived from the zoo and took Cholmondely in charge. He was marched back to his cage in disgrace, but if I know Cholmondely, he must have thought it worth any amount of scoldings just for the sight of all those people trying to get off the bus together and getting stuck in the door. Cholmondely had a great sense of humor.

From *The New Noah* by Gerald Durrell.

The Black Stallion
and
the Red Mare

by Gladys F. Lewis

At first Donald lay still. Scarcely a muscle moved. The boulders and the low shrubs screened him from view. Excitement held him motionless. His hands gripped the short grass and his toes dug into the dry earth. Cautiously he raised himself on his elbows and gazed at the scene below him.

There, in his father's unfenced hay flats, was the outlaw band of wild horses. They were grazing quietly on the rich grass. Some drank from the small hillside stream. Donald tried to count them, but they suddenly began moving about and he could not get beyond twenty. He thought there might be two hundred.

Donald knew a good deal about that band of horses, but he had never had the good luck to see them. They were known over many hundreds of square miles. They had roamed at will over the grain fields and they had led away many a domestic horse to the wild life. Once in that band, a horse was lost to the farm.

There in the flats was the great black stallion, the hero or the villain of a hundred tales. Over the far-flung prairie and grasslands there was scarcely a boy who had not dreamed of wild rides, with the great body of the stallion beneath him, bearing him clean through the air with the sharp speed of lightning.

There was the stallion now, moving among the horses with the sureness and ease of a master. As he moved about, teasingly kicking here and nipping there, a restlessness, as of a danger sensed, stirred through the band. The stallion cut to the outside of the group. At a full gallop he snaked around the wide circle, roughly bunching the mares and colts into the smaller circle of an invisible corral.

He was a magnificent creature, huge and proudly built. Donald saw the gloss of the black coat and the great

curving muscles of the strong legs, the massive hoofs, the powerful arch of the neck, the proud crest of the head. Donald imagined he could see the flash of black, intelligent eyes. Surely a nobler creature never roamed the plains!

Off-wind from the herd, a red mare came out from the fold of the low hills opposite. She stood motionless a moment, her graceful head held high. Then she nickered. The black stallion drew up short in his herding, nickered eagerly, then bolted off in the direction of the mare. She stood waiting until he had almost reached her; then they galloped back to the herd together.

The shadows crept across the hay flats and the evening stillness settled down. A bird sang sleepily on one note. Donald suddenly became aware of the monotonous song, and stirred from his intent watching. He must tell

his father and help send news around the countryside. He was still intensely excited as he crept back from the brow of the hill and hurried home. All the time his mind was busy and his heart was bursting.

Donald knew that three hundred years ago the Spaniards had brought horses to Mexico. Descendants of these horses had wandered into the Great Plains. The horses he now was watching were of that Spanish strain. Thousands of them roamed the cattle lands north to the American boundary. This band now grazed wild over these park lands here in Canada — four hundred and fifty miles north of the boundary.

His father and the farmers for many miles around had determined to round up the horses and make an end of the roving band. As a farmer's son, Donald knew that this was necessary and right. But a certain respect for the band and the fierce loyalty that he felt toward all wild, free creatures made him wish in his heart that they might never be caught, never be broken and tamed. He, who was so full of sympathy for the horses, must be traitor to them!

There had been conflicts in his heart before, but never had there been such a warring of two strong loyalties. He saw himself for the first time as a person of importance because he, Donald Turner, had the power to affect the lives of others. This power, because it could help or harm others, he knew he must use wisely.

When he stood before his father half an hour later, he did not blurt out his news. It was too important for that. But his voice and his eyes were tense with excitement. "That band of wild horses is in the hay hollow, west of the homestead quarter," he said. "There must be close to two hundred."

86

His father was aware of the boy's deep excitement. At Donald's first words he stopped his milking, his hands resting on the rim of the pail as he looked up.

"Good lad, Donald!" he said, quietly enough. "Get your supper and we'll ride to Smith's and Duncan's to start the word around. Tell Mother to pack lunches for tomorrow. We'll start at sunup." He turned to his milking again.

The other men were in the yard shortly after daylight.

Donald afterward wondered how long it would have taken ranch hands to round up the band of horses. These farmers knew horses, but not how to round up large numbers of them as the men of the ranch country knew so well. The farmers learned a good deal in the next two weeks.

Twenty men started out after the band as it thundered out of the hay flats, through the hills and over the country. The dust rose in clouds as their pounding hoofs dug the dry earth. The herd sped before the pursuers with the effortless speed of the wind. The black stallion led or drove his band, and kept them well together. That first day only the young colts were taken.

At sunset the riders unsaddled and staked their horses by a poplar thicket, ate their stale lunches and lay down to sleep under the stars. Their horses cropped the short grass and drank from the stream. Some slept standing; others lay down.

At dawn the herd was spied moving westward. With the coming of night, they, too, had rested. For a mile or more they now sped along the rim of a knoll, swift as bronchos pulled in off the range after a winter out. The

black stallion was a hundred feet ahead, running with a
tireless, easy swing, his mane and tail streaming and his
body stretched level as it cut through the morning mists.
Close at his side, but half a length behind him, ran the
red mare. The band streamed after.

After the first day's chase and the night under the
stars, Donald had ridden back home. Not that he had
wanted to go back. He would have given everything that
he owned to have gone on with the men. But there were
horses and cattle and chores to attend to at home, and
there was school.

The roundup continued. Each day saw the capture of more and more horses. As the men doubled back on their course, they began to see that the wild horses traveled in a great circle, coming back again and again over the same ground, stopping at the same watering holes and feeding in the same rich grass flats. Once this course became clear, fresh riders and mounts in relays were posted along the way, while others drove on from behind. The wild band had still to press on with little chance for rest and feeding. The strain of the pursuit took away their desire for food, but they had a burning thirst and the black stallion would never let them drink their fill before he drove them on. Fatigue grew on them.

As the roundup continued, the whole countryside stirred with excitement. At every town where there was a grain elevator along the railroad, people repeated the latest news of the chase. On the farms the hay went unmown or unraked, and the plows rested still in the last furrow of the summer fallow. At school the children played roundup at recess. Donald, at his desk, saw the printed pages of his books, but his mind was miles away, running with the now almost exhausted wild horses.

Near the end of the second week of the chase, Donald's father rode into the yard. Donald dropped the wood he was carrying to the house and ran to meet his father.

"Dad, they haven't got the black stallion and the red mare, have they?" Donald could scarcely wait for his father's slow reply.

"No, Donald, lad," he said. "Though those two are the only horses still free. They're back in the flats. We'll get them tomorrow."

Donald felt both relief and fear.

In the yellow lamplight of the supper table his father told of the long days of riding, of the farms where he had eaten and rested, and of the adventures of each day.

"That was a gallant band, lad!" he said. "Never shall we see their equal! Those two that are left are a pair of great horses. Most wild horses show a weakening in the strain and grow up with little wind or muscle. But these two are sound of wind and their muscles are like steel. Besides that, they have intelligence. They would have been taken long ago but for that."

No one spoke. Donald felt that his father was on his side, the side of the horses. After a long pause, Mr. Turner continued.

"With his brains and his strength, that stallion could have got away in the very beginning. He could have got away a dozen times and would now be free south of the border. But that was his band. He stayed by them, and he tried to get them to safety. This week, when his band had been rounded up, he stuck by that red mare. She is swift but she can't match his speed. It's curious the way they keep together! He stops and nickers. She nickers in reply and comes close to him, her nose touching his flank. They stand a moment. Then they are away again, she running beside him but not quite neck to neck. Day after day it is the same. They are no ordinary horseflesh, those two, lad!"

There was a lump in Donald's throat. He knew what his father meant. Those horses seemed to stand for something bigger and greater than himself. There were other things that made him feel the same — the first full-throated song of the meadow lark in the spring; ripe golden fields of wheat with the breeze rippling it in waves; the sun setting over the rim of the world in a blaze of rose and gold; the sun rising again in the quiet east; the smile in the blue depths of his mother's eyes; the still whiteness of the snow-bound plains; the story of Columbus dauntlessly sailing off into unknown seas.

These things were part of a hidden, exciting world. The boy belonged to these things in some strange way. He caught only glimpses of that hidden world, but those glimpses were tantalizing. Something deep within him leaped up in joy.

That night Donald dreamed of horses nickering to him, but when he tried to find them, they were no longer there. Then he dreamed that he was riding the great, black stallion, riding over a far-flung range, riding along a hilltop road with the world spread below him on every side. He felt the powerful body of the horse beneath him. He felt the smooth curves of the mighty muscles. Horse and rider seemed as one.

A cold dawn shattered his glorious dream ride. With his father he joined the other horsemen. From the crest of the slope from which Donald had first seen them, the pair of horses was sighted. They were dark, moving shadows in the gray mists of the morning.

They had just finished drinking deep from the stream. Not for two weeks had the men seen the horses drink like that. Thirsty as they were, they had taken but one drink at each water hole. This last morning they were jaded and spent; they had thrown caution to the winds.

At the first suspicion of close danger, they stood still, heads and tails erect. Then they dashed toward the protecting hills. There the way forked.

It was then Donald saw happen the strange thing his father had described. At the fork the stallion halted and nickered. The mare answered and came close. She touched his flank with her head. Then they bounded off and disappeared in the path that led northwest to the rougher country where the chase had not led before.

Along the way the horses had been expected to take, grain-fed horses had been stationed. These had now to move over northwest. But the men were in no hurry today. They were sure of the take before nightfall. The sun was low in the west when two riders spurred their mounts for the close-in. The stallion and the mare were

not a hundred yards ahead. They were dead spent. Their
glossy coats were flecked with dark foam. Fatigue showed
in every line of their bodies. Their gallant spirits no longer
could drive their spent bodies. The stallion called to the
mare. He heard her answer behind him. He slowed down,
turning wildly in every direction. She came up to him;
her head drooped on his flank and rested there. In a last
wild defiance, the stallion tossed his magnificent head and
drew strength for a last mighty effort. Too late!

The smooth coils of a rope tightened around his feet. He was down, down and helpless. He saw the mare fall as the rope slipped over her body and drew tight around her legs. It maddened him. He struggled wildly to be free. The taut rope held. The stallion was conquered. In that last struggle something went out of him. Broken was his body and broken was his spirit. Never again would he roam the plains, proud and free, the monarch of his herd.

Donald saw it all. He felt it all. His hands gripped the pommel of the saddle and his knees pressed hard against his pony's side. Tears blinded his eyes and from his throat came the sound of a single sob. It was as if he himself were being broken and tied.

The sun dipped below the rim of the plains. The day was gone; the chase was ended. The men stood about smoking and talking in groups of two's and three's, examining the two roped horses. Donald's father knelt close to the mare, watching her intently. Donald watched him. His father remained quiet for a moment, one knee still resting on the ground, in his hand his unsmoked pipe.

Donald waited for his father to speak. At last the words came.

"Boys," he said, without looking up, and with measured words, "do you know, this mare is blind — stone blind!"

A week later, Donald and his father stood watching those two horses in the Turner corral. They were not the same spirited creatures, but they were still magnificent horses.

"I figured," his father said, turning to the boy, "that they had won the right to stay together. I've brought them home for you, Donald. They are yours, lad. I know you will be good to them."

Food for Wolves

by Farley Mowat

Canadian biologist Farley Mowat, sent by his government to study the diet of the wolves in the Keewatin Barren Lands of northern Canada, tells about watching the summer hunting activities of three wolves. He has given the wolves the names George, Angeline, and Uncle Albert.

After some weeks of study I still seemed to be as far as ever from solving the problem of how the wolves made a living during the summer.

Toward the end of June the last of the migrating caribou herds had passed Wolf House Bay, heading for the high Barrens some two or three hundred miles to the north, where they would spend the summer.

Whatever my wolves were going to eat during those long months and whatever they were going to feed their hungry pups, it would not be caribou, for the caribou were gone. But if not caribou, what *was* it to be?

I checked off all the other possibilities I could think of, but there seemed to be no source of food available which would be adequate to satisfy the appetites of three

adult and four young wolves. Apart from myself (and the thought recurred several times) there was hardly an animal left in the country which could be considered suitable prey for a wolf. Arctic hares were present; but they were very scarce and so fleet of foot that a wolf could not hope to catch one unless he was extremely lucky. Ptarmigan and other birds were numerous; but they could fly, and the wolves could not. Lake trout, arctic grayling, and whitefish filled the lakes and rivers; but wolves are not otters.

The days passed and the mystery deepened. To make the problem even more inscrutable, the wolves seemed reasonably well fed; and to baffle me to the point of near insanity, the two male wolves went off hunting every night and returned every morning, but never appeared to bring anything home.

As far as I could tell, the whole lot of them seemed to be existing on a diet of air and water. Once, moved by a growing concern for their well-being, I went back to the cabin and baked five loaves of bread, which I then took to Wolf House Bay and left beside one of the hunting paths. My gift was rejected.

About this time I began having trouble with mice. The vast expanses of spongy sphagnum bog provided ideal surroundings for several species of small rodents who could burrow and nest-build to their hearts' content in the ready-made mattress of moss. They had litters of young too, and they must have had them with great frequency, for as June waned into July the country seemed to become alive with little rodents. Red-backed mice and meadow mice began invading the cabin in such numbers that it looked as if *I* would soon be starving unless I could thwart their appetites for my supplies. *They* did not scorn my bread. They did not scorn my bed either; and I awoke one morning to find that a meadow mouse had given birth to eleven naked offspring inside the pillow of my sleeping bag.

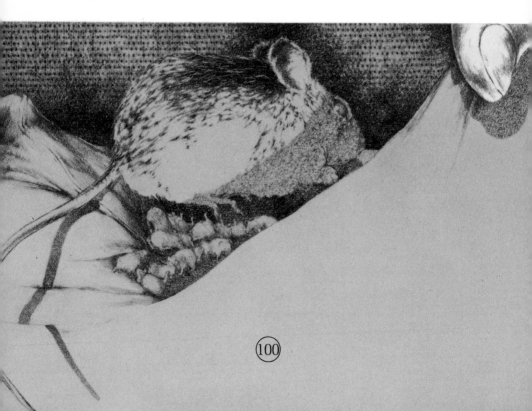

I suppose it was only because my own wolf indoctrination had been so complete, and of such an inaccurate nature, that it took me so long to account for the healthy state of the wolves in the apparent absence of any game worthy of their reputation and physical abilities. The idea of wolves not only eating, but actually thriving and raising their families on a diet of mice was so at odds with the character of the mythical wolf that it was really too ridiculous to consider. And yet, it was the answer to the problem of how my wolves were keeping the larder full.

Angeline tipped me off.

Late one afternoon, while the male wolves were still resting in preparation for the night's labors, she emerged from the den and nuzzled Uncle Albert until he yawned, stretched, and got laboriously to his feet. Then she left the den site at a trot, heading directly for me across a broad expanse of grassy bog, and leaving Albert to entertain the pups as best he could.

There was nothing particularly new in this. I had several times seen her enlist Albert (and on rare occasions even George) to do duty as a babysitter while she went down to the bay for a drink or, as I mistakenly thought, simply went for a walk to stretch her legs. Usually her wanderings took her to the point of the bay farthest from my tent where she was hidden from sight by a low gravel ridge; but this time she came my way in full view and so I swung my telescope to keep an eye on her.

She went directly to the rocky foreshore, waded out until the icy water was up to her shoulders, and had a long drink. As she was doing so, a small flock of Old Squaw ducks flew around the point of the bay and pitched only a hundred yards or so away from her. She raised her head and eyed them thoughtfully for a moment, then waded back to shore, where she proceeded to act as if she had suddenly gone mad.

Yipping like a puppy, she began to chase her tail, to roll over and over among the rocks, to lie on her back, to wave all four feet furiously in the air, and in general to behave as if she were clean out of her mind.

I swung the glasses back to where Albert was sitting amidst a gaggle of pups to see if he, too, had observed this mad display, and, if so, what his reaction to it was. He had seen it all right; in fact he was watching Angeline with keen interest but without the slightest indication of alarm.

By this time Angeline was leaping wildly into the air and snapping at nothing, all the while uttering shrill squeals. It was an awe-inspiring sight, and I realized that

Albert and I were not the only ones who were watching it with fascination. The ducks seemed hypnotized by curiosity. So interested were they that they swam in for a closer view of this strange sight on the shore. Closer and closer they came, necks outstretched, and gabbling disbelievingly among themselves. And the closer they came, the crazier grew Angeline's behavior.

When the leading duck was not more than fifteen feet from shore, Angeline gave one gigantic leap towards it. There was a vast splash, a panic-striken whacking of wings, and then all the ducks were up and away. Angeline had missed a dinner by no more than inches.

This incident was an eye-opener since it suggested a talent for food-getting which I would hardly have credited to a human being, let alone to a mere wolf. However,

Angeline soon demonstrated that the charming of ducks was a mere side line.

Having dried herself with a series of energetic shakes which momentarily hid her in a blue mist of water droplets, she padded back across the grassy swale. But now her movements were quite different from what they had been when she passed through the swale on the way to the bay.

Angeline was of a rangy build, anyway, but by stretching herself so that she seemed to be walking on tiptoe, and by elevating her neck like a camel, she seemed to gain several inches in height. She began to move infinitely slowly upwind across the swale, and I had the impression that both ears were cocked for the faintest sound, while I could see her nose wrinkling as she sifted the breeze for the most delicate scents.

Suddenly she pounced. Flinging herself up on her hind legs like a horse trying to throw its rider, she came down again with driving force, both forelegs held stiffly out in front of her. Instantly her head dropped; she snapped once, swallowed, and returned to her peculiar mincing ballet across the swale. Six times in ten minutes she repeated the straight-armed pounce, and six times she swallowed — without my having caught a glimpse of what it was that she had eaten. The seventh time she missed her aim, spun around, and began snapping frenziedly in a tangle of cotton grasses. This time when she raised her head I saw, quite unmistakably, the tail and hind quarters of a mouse quivering in her jaws. One gulp, and it too was gone.

Although I was much entertained by the spectacle of one of this continent's most powerful carnivores hunting mice, I did not really take it seriously. I thought Angeline

was only having fun; snacking, as it were. But when she had eaten some twenty-three mice, I began to wonder. Mice are small, but twenty-three of them add up to a fair-sized meal, even for a wolf.

It was only later, by putting two and two together, that I was able to bring myself to an acceptance of the obvious. The wolves of Wolf House Bay, and, by my guess at least, all the Barren Land wolves who were raising families outside the summer caribou range, were living largely, if not almost entirely, on mice.

Only one point remained obscure and that was how they transported the catch of mice (which in the course of an entire night must have amounted to a formidable number of individuals) back to the dens to feed the pups.

I never did solve this problem until I met some neighboring Eskimos. One of them, a charming fellow named Ootek, who became a close friend (and who was a first-rate, if untrained, naturalist), explained the mystery.

Since it was impossible for the wolves to carry the mice home externally, they did the next best thing and brought them home in their bellies. I had already noticed that when either George or Albert returned from a hunt they went straight to the den and crawled into it. Though I did not suspect it at the time, they were regurgitating the day's rations, already partially digested.

Later in the summer, when the pups had abandoned the den, I several times saw one of the adult wolves regurgitating a meal for them. However, if I had not known what they were doing I probably would have misunderstood the action and still been no whit the wiser as to how the wolves carried home their spoils.

From *Never Cry Wolf* by Farley Mowat.

For Further Reading

BOOKS

City Critters
by *Helen R. Russell*

Elsa *(or the original book,* Born Free*)*
by *Joy Adamson*

Elsa and Her Cubs *(or the original book,* Living Free*)*
by *Joy Adamson*

How to Understand Animal Talk
by *Vinson Brown*

The Misunderstood Skunk
by *Lilo Hess*

My Dear Dolphin
by *Cynthia de Narvaez*

Rascal
by *Sterling North*

Ring of Bright Water *(young reader's edition)*
by *Gavin Maxwell*

Squirrels in the Garden
by *Olive L. Earle*

The True Story of Okee the Otter
by *Dorothy Wisbeski*

MAGAZINES

Animals

Animal Kingdom

The Curious Naturalist

Ranger Rick's Nature Magazine

Next, see "Keep an Animal Log" and "Write Your Own Animal Story" in FINDING OUT, "Make an Animal" and "Map a Zoo or Park" in MAKING THINGS, "Sharing Reading" in TELLING ABOUT, and "Who's Talking?" in MAKING UP.

Stories on circled ◯ pages have been recorded. Look for them under *Animal Stories, True* in the LISTENING LIBRARY.

Art Credits
Ben Stahl: cover.
Carl Burger: pages iv – 6.
Les Morrill: pages 8 – 15, 44 – 59.
Bill Peet: pages 16 – 29.
Roy Combs: pages 30 – 41.
Den Schoenfeld: pages 60 – 68.
Fred Gerlach: pages 70 – 81, 96 – 105.
Suzanne Valla: pages 82 – 95.

ABCDEFGHIJ–VF–7809876543 2